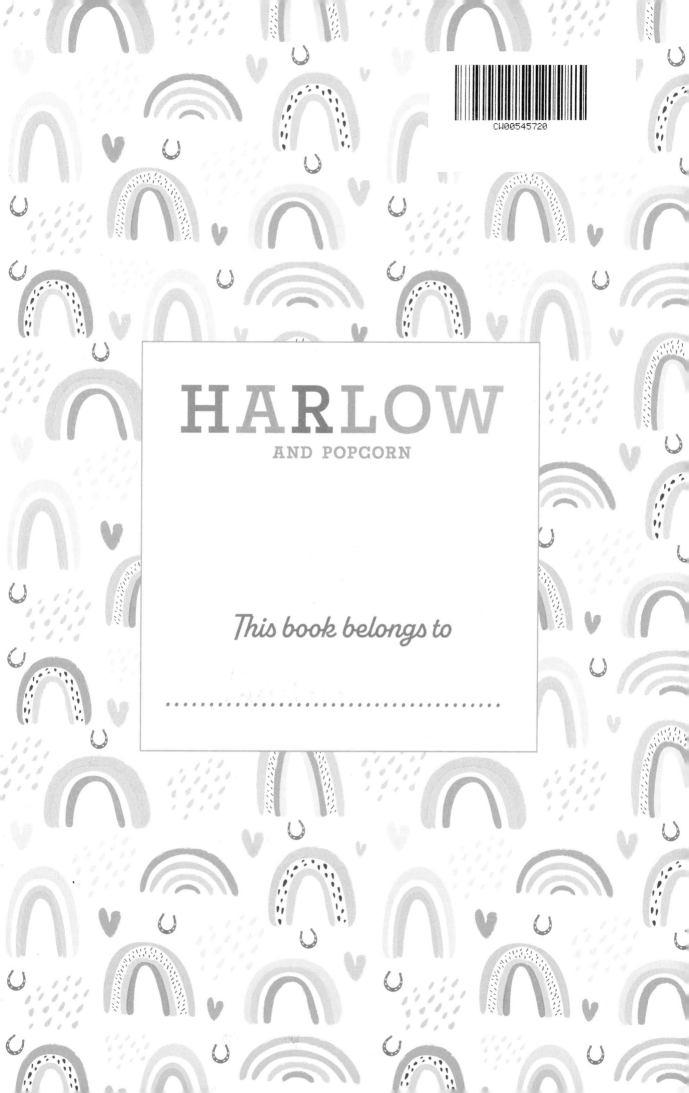

HARLOW
AND POPCORN

This book belongs to

....

HARLOW
AND POPCORN
Contents

HARLOW
AND POPCORN

Published by DJ Murphy (Publishers) Ltd, Olive Studio, Grange Road, Tilford, Farnham, Surrey GU10 2DQ

Who did what in Harlow Yearbook 2023
Harlow Luna White
Contributors Helen Barker-Benfield, Kiera Boyle, Sarah Burgess, Louise Kittle
Head of Art and Design Sarah Garland
Designers Jake Booth, Paul Smail, Adam Witt
Lifestyle photographers Peter Nixon, Chelsea White
Managing Director Zoe Cannon
Commercial Director Abi Cannon

Harlow Yearbook is produced under license by DJ Murphy (Publishers) Ltd.
© Copyright DJ Murphy (Publishers) Ltd.

Printed by Graphicom via dell'Industria – 36100 Vicenza, Italy

ISBN 978-1-913787-12-7

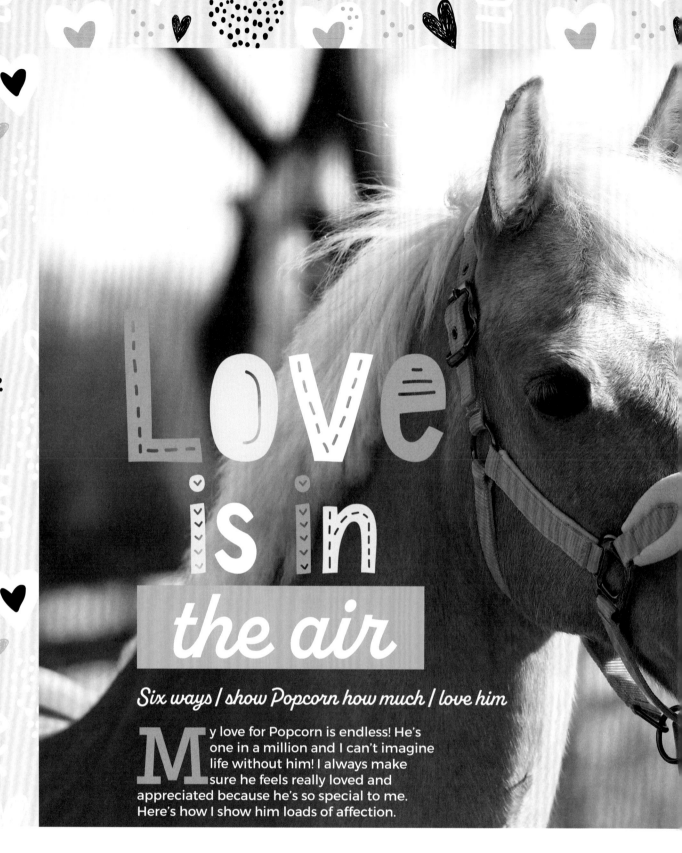

Love is in the air

Six ways I show Popcorn how much I love him

My love for Popcorn is endless! He's one in a million and I can't imagine life without him! I always make sure he feels really loved and appreciated because he's so special to me. Here's how I show him loads of affection.

Bear hug
Who doesn't love pony cuddles? It's so cute watching Popcorn have a snooze and I can't help but wrap my arms around him and give him a big kiss! The feeling of Popcorn's smooth, silky coat against my skin is the best.

Munchies
Popcorn's fave treat is a carrot – he goes crazy for them! So, when he's been a really good boy after a mega jumping session or has strolled over to me in the field, he gets a delicious carrot as a reward. Lucky boy!

Spa day
Booking an appointment for Popcorn with a massage therapist is the perfect way to make him feel great. Not only will he be super-supple and flexible afterwards, but he'll also feel relaxed and ready for our next outing!

THE LOWDOWN

Spend time getting to know your pony, including his likes and dislikes, so you can show him how much he means to you! Enjoying quality time together is a great way to boost your bond and will make your pony more happy to do whatever you ask of him.

♡ ♡ ♡

THE LOWDOWN

Ponies communicate with us through their body language, so watch out for signs that'll show how your pony feels while you're giving him attention. If he's happy, he'll prick his ears forwards, if he's feeling relaxed you might notice he has a droopy bottom lip and if he's upset, he might swish his tail or put his ears back.

♡ ♡ ♡

Adventure time

Popcorn loves jumping, going to the gallops and playing in the field! And when I want to show him some extra love, I'll take him on a fun adventure and watch his ears prick forwards and face light up with happiness.

Tickle monster

Isn't it so funny and cute when your pony wobbles his lip when you find his fave scratchy spot? Popcorn loves being scratched on his withers and tries to groom me back – a sure sign he's feeling the love!

Super-spoilt

A pamper session is the ultimate way to show your pony some love. There's nothing like spending time making him sparkle all over – why not check out my guides to grooming and bathing on pages 22 and 54?

AROUND THE WORLD

Spin around in your saddle and take on this dizzying dare!

What?

Around the world is when you do a full 360° turn, moving one leg at a time to turn your body, while sitting on a pony. You might think it's just a fun game to play, but it's a tricky challenge that tests your balance and core strength – two essential things for riding. It's also really easy to slip off, especially if you're having a go while bareback and your pony's coat is shiny!

How?

Once you get the hang of around the world, it's super-easy, but take your time at first so you don't slip off the side or spook your pony. Here's how I do it...

1. I halt Popcorn in the arena and ask my mum to hold onto him, then I cross over my stirrups and make a knot in my reins.
2. I lift my left leg over Popcorn's neck so both legs are on his right-hand side.
3. Then, my right leg goes over his hindquarters so I'm facing backwards – at this point I'm hoping Popcorn stands still!
4. Next, I bring my left leg over, too, so my legs are now hanging down Popcorn's left-hand side.
5. Finally, I lift my right leg over Popcorn's neck so I end up facing forwards and in a normal riding position!

HEARD IT FROM HARLOW

I always try this challenge clockwise and anti-clockwise! It helps to check my balance and strength in both directions – which, surprisingly, can differ loads!

If your pony's nervous or spooky, have a go at just lifting one leg over the saddle and sitting sideways first, rather than trying around the world straight away. He might feel really unsure if you're suddenly sitting backwards, so make sure he's happy at each stage before you progress.

Fun

⁝ TRY YOURSELF ⁝

Have a go at around the world at the end of a fun riding lesson or schedule in a session with your friends to race against each other! See who can do it the quickest, and try doing it clockwise and then anti-clockwise straight away – it might make you feel a bit dizzy, but it's super-fun!

SOMEWHERE OVER THE
Rainbow

After some colourful riding outfit inspo? Then look no further!
Here's how I wear the rainbow

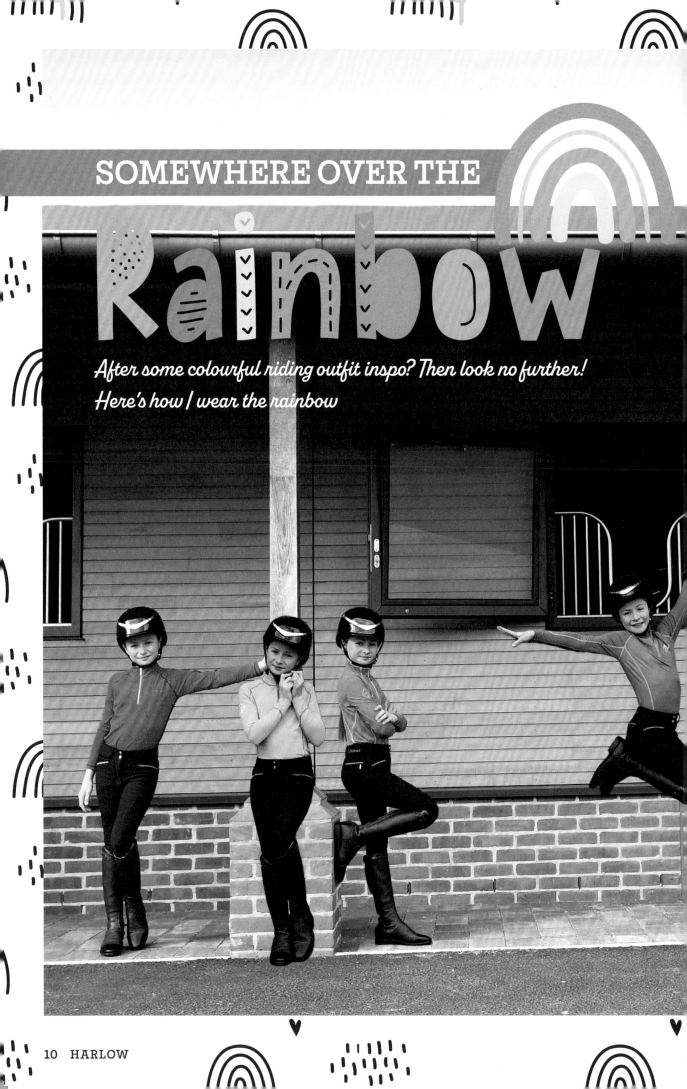

Why I love...
Hacking
in the forest

Wandering in the woods and stopping off for ice cream, how can I not love hacking in the forest?

Positive vibes

Riding in the forest has done wonders for Popcorn's responsiveness, which has boosted our confidence in the school, too. Going from quiet tracks to big open spaces means he really has to listen to my aids and I have to keep him focused so he's always paying attention to me.

Snack attack

Our hacks through the forest are usually pretty long, so we always take snacks or stop off to refill our tanks along the way! It's so much fun going for a picnic with our friends or grabbing an ice cream from the van. Popcorn enjoys a haynet when we stop off for lunch, too!

Open up

When we find the perfect spot for a gallop, I encourage Popcorn to canter and he pricks his ears to show his delight! Letting him stretch out and have a blast gives me such an adrenaline rush!

Peace and quiet

In between the super-fun and fast parts of our hacks in the forest, I love taking in the beautiful scenery around me as we stroll through the woods. Tuning in to the beat of Popcorn's hooves on the ground beneath, as well as the birds singing in the trees, makes me feel so calm and content – it's pure bliss!

Super social

I'm so lucky to be able to go on loads of adventures with Popcorn and our friends. We have so much fun together when hacking – we sing our fave songs, tell each other funny stories and, most importantly, plan our next big outing!

It's always a good idea to call out to walkers to let them know you're approaching and be sure to slow down as you ride past them and other horses – you don't want to spook them!

THE LOWDOWN

You can ride on bridleways and byways, but not on footpaths, so look out for signposts to make sure you're following the right track!

PERFECT POLEWORK

Climb up the levels to progress your polework skills

Polework's so handy because it has endless benefits for your pony. It can help to improve his co-ordination, strength and flexibility – plus, it's a super-fun way to spice up your usual schooling sessions!

Level one

Whenever I have a polework session, I start with the basics and ride over walk, trot and canter poles. I set out four poles 0.5–0.8m apart for walk, 1–1.2m for trot and 2.7–3m for canter. As I approach the poles, I make sure Popcorn's in front of my leg and moving forward, and that I'm looking up. I channel him straight with my hands and legs to get a good approach, too!

Tick when completed

Level two

The zig-zag exercise is a great accuracy test! I put out five poles to create a zig-zag, making sure the distance between the middle of each pole is equal. I'll use this exercise to keep Popcorn's rhythm and straightness in check – if he drifts to one side of the poles, it'll throw the distances out of sync so I have to make sure I ride him really accurately.

Tick when completed

THE LOWDOWN

Horses usually have much longer strides than ponies, but that doesn't mean all ponies will have the exact same stride length. So, keep your pony in mind when setting out pole distances – if he has a really short or long stride, you'll need to adjust the distance to suit him.

Level three

Next, I use four poles to create a fan shape, measuring from the middle of each one and using the same distances as if they were in a straight line. I use my inside rein to ask Popcorn to bend and I support him with my outside rein and leg to prevent him falling out – this exercise is hard work, so I stick to walk and build up to trot and canter when we feel confident and ready.

Tick when completed

Next level

♡ ♡ ♡

Looking to give your polework skills an even bigger boost? Why not up the difficulty by raising some of the poles slightly using small blocks or adjust the distances a little bit to encourage your pony to shorten or lengthen his strides to suit? Don't forget, you'll need to use strong riding aids to help him!

Level four

I use 10 poles to create the sweetie – it's the ultimate polework exercise that tests a whole bunch of different skills! There are loads of ways to ride through it – my three faves are riding from one end to the other to check straightness, diagonally over the points of the square to test accuracy and over the two triangle ends, which create a circle to encourage Popcorn to be supple.

Tick when completed

Happy as a horse

Do you know what ponies need to feel good?
Here are four things they love!

Keeping Popcorn happy and healthy is my biggest priority. So, I do everything I can and provide him with all the things he loves and needs to keep him on top form and living his best life!

Field day
It might be hard to believe, but ponies can walk up to 18 miles a day in the wild! So, to keep our ponies really happy, we should always make sure they have plenty of regular access to a field. That way, they have freedom to move around, graze, relax and play with their friends.

Tummy time
In the wild, ponies spend a whopping 16–18 hours each day grazing – how crazy is that? This is why we need to feed them little and often because they've evolved to be trickle feeders. Like me, ponies love sweet treats, such as apples and mints! But their gut needs lots of forage to work correctly. Popcorn only gets his fave treats as a reward when he's done a good job because too many can upset his stomach and make him more likely to become overweight. That definitely wouldn't keep him happy!

Brilliant bonds
Ponies are really sociable animals and live in herds in the wild. They communicate using body language and enjoy building friendships with their herd mates through mutual grooming. This is when two ponies groom each other's back and withers with their teeth and muzzle – it's super-cute. Scratching your pony in his fave itchy spot is like mutual grooming, which will make him feel really calm and happy!

Sweet dreams
Even though ponies are designed to spend most of their day grazing, they love taking naps, too! Did you know a pony will only sleep for around three hours each day, though? It's amazing how they can perform so well on such little sleep! Whenever I catch Popcorn having some quiet time, I can't resist taking a pic and chilling out with him – it's so adorable!

- THE LOWDOWN -

To maintain condition, ponies need to eat 2% of their bodyweight in dry forage every day. It's really important you don't feed your pony less than 1.5% of his bodyweight – even if you're trying to help him stay trim – otherwise he might become poorly. And no poorly pony is happy!

- THE LOWDOWN -

Ponies usually snooze standing up due to their natural flight instinct. Standing up means that if they're in danger, they can get to safety much quicker than if they're lying down! But to get essential REM sleep – where they can dream – they need to be lying down. However he's sleeping, you know a sleeping pony is a relaxed, happy one!

HEARD IT FROM HARLOW

For most of the year Popcorn lives in his stable at night and goes out in the field during the day. But if it's really warm in summer, he gets to go out overnight and stays in his stable during the day to keep cool and comfortable!

Celebrate

HAPPY BIRTHDAY

Give your fave pony the birthday he deserves with my guide for celebrating his special day!

All about him

On your pony's birthday, you've got to celebrate everything amazing about him and give him loads of attention! So, plan your time around his fave activities to make sure he has the best day ever. Here are some ideas...

- let him have an extra hour in the field with his best equine pals
- organise a fun adventure to his special place – it could be the beach, the woods or the XC course!
- go for a hack and enjoy a canter along his fave stretch of grass
- have a jumping lesson!
- book a session with your physio to make him feel really good
- get him gleaming, then have a photoshoot to mark the occasion!

Get the look

You could choose your outfit for the day based on your fave matchy set or be inspired by his name, like me! I wore a super-cute popcorn dress for Popcorn's birthday last year – it was perfect! If your fave pony suits a range of colours, why not go all out and wear a rainbow of the colours that suit him? It's always so much fun playing around with outfits to celebrate his birthday!

OH, SO EXTRA!

Take it to the max and celebrate your pony's birthday in style with these added extras...

- [ ] decorate around his stable with bunting, balloons and banners
- [ ] attach a party hat to your riding helmet so everyone knows you're celebrating!
- [ ] create a cake out of his fave treat – you could even sing happy birthday as you give it to him!
- [ ] get all his best pals together and throw him a special party on the yard

HEARD IT FROM HARLOW

Grooming Popcorn every day helps keep him in top condition, but on his birthday I like to spoil him with a mega pamper session. This includes a massage under the solarium and a thorough groom. Plus, a tonne of extra cuddles and loads of scratches in his fave itchy spot!

PERFECTLY

PAMPERED

How I turn Popcorn from a muddy monster
to a pristine pony in six easy steps!

I love treating Popcorn to a nice, long pamper session, but I don't always have time to give him a thorough groom after school. Daily grooming is an important part of pony care, but if I need to get on and ride, I keep things simple. Here's how...

KIT CHECK

- ☐ hoof pick
- ☐ dandy brush
- ☐ rubber curry comb
- ☐ body brush
- ☐ metal curry comb
- ☐ sponge
- ☐ mane and tail brush
- ☐ detangling spray
- ☐ hoof oil
- ☐ coat shine and cloth

Let's go

1. First of all, I pick out Popcorn's feet to remove all the bedding and mud by working downwards from heel to toe and taking care around his frog.

2. Next, I use my dandy brush or rubber curry comb on his muddy areas to loosen the dirt and help remove any hair that's coming out.

3. Now I grab my body brush and use it in short sweeping motions all over Popcorn's body in the direction of his coat. I clean the dirt and dust off the brush using my metal curry comb.

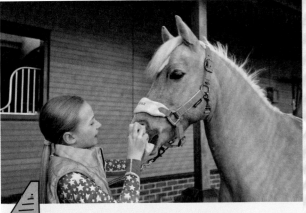

4. I gently place one hand on Popcorn's head to keep him still and, with the brush in my other hand, carefully brush his face. If his eyes, nose and muzzle are a bit dirty, I'll grab a damp sponge and gently wipe over them.

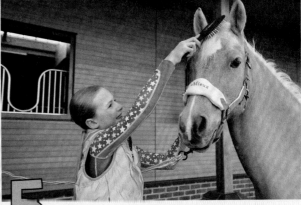

5. Next, I brush through his mane, tail and forelock. Using detangling spray helps to get rid of any knots easily and gives his hair a glossy look.

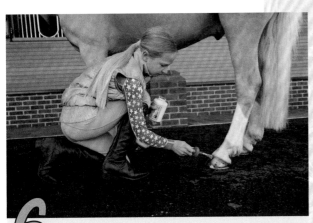

6. Finally, I make his hooves shine with hoof oil and spray some coat shine onto a cloth, which I then wipe over his body – it's the ultimate finish!

THE LOWDOWN

How thoroughly you should groom your pony depends on his routine! If he lives out, it's best to avoid grooming him too much because it'll remove a large amount of the natural oils in his coat that he needs to help keep him warm and dry. Whereas, if he's stable-kept or rugged a lot, giving him a good groom each day will help stop dirt building up.

THE LOWDOWN

Mutual grooming's when ponies stand together and scratch each other with their teeth and lips. It can strengthen their friendship as well as help to remove loose hair and dead skin – just like when you groom your pony!

Nailed it

Now your pony's groomed to perfection and is shining from head to toe, why not have a fun photoshoot with him? It's the perfect chance to get some beautiful pics of him – or the two of you together – while he's looking 10/10!

HEARD IT FROM HARLOW

I groom Popcorn every day and use the time to carefully check him over for any lumps, bumps or changes that might need extra attention.

Make Popcorn holder!

Follow my easy step-by-step guide to create your own!

Whether you're off on a horsey day out, watching a friend's lesson or just snuggling up on the sofa for a movie night at home, take my adorable popcorn holder along with you. Simply fill with yummy treats, sit back and enjoy the action!

Kit check
- ☐ popcorn template
- ☐ card
- ☐ scissors
- ☐ glue stick
- ☐ your fave snacks!

Let's go

1. Print out my cute Harlow and Popcorn template – to download it, visit **bit.ly/POPCORN_BOX**

2. Stick the template onto a piece of card – this will give your holder a more solid structure.

3. Carefully cut around the edge of the popcorn holder, along the dotted line. Ask an adult for help if you need it!

4. Fold along all the lines so the pink tabs and four sides of the holder are scored.

5. Run your glue stick along the long pink tab and stick to the inside of the other end to create the oblong shape. Then, fold the bottom tabs over each other and glue together.

6. Once it's dry, all you need to do is fill up your popcorn holder with your fave snacks – mine's obviously popcorn – and enjoy!

HEARD IT FROM HARLOW

Don't worry if you don't have a printer, you can trace the template on page 101 and colour in your own design! You could draw some funky, colourful patterns or paint a picture of a pony. Whether you use my design or your own, it's sure to look phenom!

The PLACE to be

Ponies, pals and the great outdoors – this is why the yard is totally awesome

The yard's easily the best place in the world and I love spending time there! We're super-lucky and have access to so many amazing facilities, but there's much more than that to being at the stables.

Horsey haven

The yard is where our trusty four-legged friends live, so it's no wonder it's our favourite place to be! The list of things to do with your fave pony at the stables is endless and, if you're like me, you'll never get bored of hanging out with him. Plus, helping him feel good and watching him enjoy life is really amazing.

Pony-mad pals

Me and my friends always have so much fun at the yard – we play games, spend hours setting up courses and jumping around the arena on foot and in summer, go blackberry picking! It's so nice to have a group of pals who are pony-mad and love being around them as much as I do.

THE LOWDOWN

If you're on the hunt for a new yard or you're about to get your first pony, make sure you consider the yard's routine in comparison to your pony's current one and how it'll affect his happiness. It can be really difficult to handle a pony who hasn't settled into his environment, so always put his needs first.

Light, airy stables are so dreamy

THE LOWDOWN

Not all yards will have loads of hacking on their doorstep, indoor schools to shelter you from the elements or gallops to help keep your pony ultra-fit, and that doesn't matter. The most important thing is that your pony's basic needs are met – field, friends and food – and that you can enjoy your time with him there!

Tack room goals!

Nature's finest

After what feels like a lifetime sat in the classroom, there's nothing better than stepping out into the fresh air and spending time with your fave pony. Whether I'm going for a fun ride on a warm, summer's evening or taking Popcorn for a graze in-hand, the calming vibe I get from being out in the countryside makes me feel so happy.

Superb skills

There's so much to learn about ponies! You can do loads of learning away from the stables, through watching YouTube videos and pros at events or reading books and magazines at home. But the yard is the place you can put all your horsey knowledge and skills into practise.

On the road!

Get ready to travel with me and Popcorn as we explore the big, wide world!

DEAR DIARY

I love planning pony adventures with my mum! Organising a proper schedule for our outings helps us feel prepared so the day runs smoothly!

I can't live without checklists – make one and stick it to your tack locker so you don't forget to pack anything important!

THE LOWDOWN

Whether a pony's travelling down the road for a schooling session or going a few hours away for a stay-away show, the law says he must always travel with his passport.

FIRST-CLASS SERVICE

Before loading Popcorn onto the horsebox, I make up a haynet so he can have a snack on the journey. I also make sure we have a bucket, plenty of fresh water and a spare haynet for him, as well as other travelling essentials, such as a first aid kit and our tack!

WALK-IN WARDROBE

Popcorn's travelling gear makes him look super-smart and also helps to keep him safe. When we're getting ready to go out in the horsebox, I always put on his travel boots, tail guard and leather headcollar. Depending on the weather, I might pop on his fancy show rug, too!

THE LOWDOWN

Did you know travelling can be hard work for a pony? He'll use almost the same amount of energy travelling for an hour as he would if he was walking for that long! So, make sure you plan in plenty of breaks if you're going on a long journey.

TAKE CARE

Mum's always on hand to help me with Popcorn, but I need kit to help keep me safe while I'm loading and unloading him. So, I always make sure I'm wearing my riding hat, gloves and a pair of sturdy boots.

Meet Harlow

FACT-FILE

- **DATE OF BIRTH**
  1 September 2011
- **HEIGHT**
  4ft 7ins
- **BEST HORSEY FRIEND**
  Lexi
- **FAVE SNACK**
  Popcorn!
- **FAVE ACTIVITY**
  Anything to do with ponies!
- **BEST COLOUR**
  Pink

The first time I ever sat on a pony was when I was just two years old! It was my mum's pony, Houdini, and I loved it so much – I was hooked!

When I was nine, Mum finally agreed to buy me my own pony, and along came Popcorn! He was the first and only pony we tried – it's like we were made for each other because we instantly clicked.

When I'm at home, I love to play pony games on my iPad, like Star Stable and Rival Stars Horse Racing, or play with my Schleich ponies. But, if I'm having a non-horsey day, I enjoy going to the gym for a swim, run and a quick blast around the soft play area – you're never too old for that!

Social superstar

My first YouTube video with Popcorn was a series of clips from our first two weeks together. We didn't expect the reaction that we got, but the views steadily increased, and when they reached 20,000, I was completely blown away. It felt incredible!

Insider info

My fave subject at school is definitely English! I love to read and write stories. Plus, my teacher's the best!

"It's like we were made for each other because we instantly clicked"

HEARD IT FROM HARLOW

My fave ice cream flavour is mint choc chip – nothing can beat it! Plus, if it's in a crunchy waffle cone it's even better! What's your favourite ice cream combo?

HEARD IT FROM HARLOW

On a normal week I see Popcorn four times – both weekend days and twice during the week after school. I miss him so much on the days I can't go to the yard, but it makes it more special when we get quality time together.

Look into the future

What discipline are you destined for?

Have you ever wondered what the future holds for you and your fave pony? Take my fun quiz to find out which sport you'll excel at!

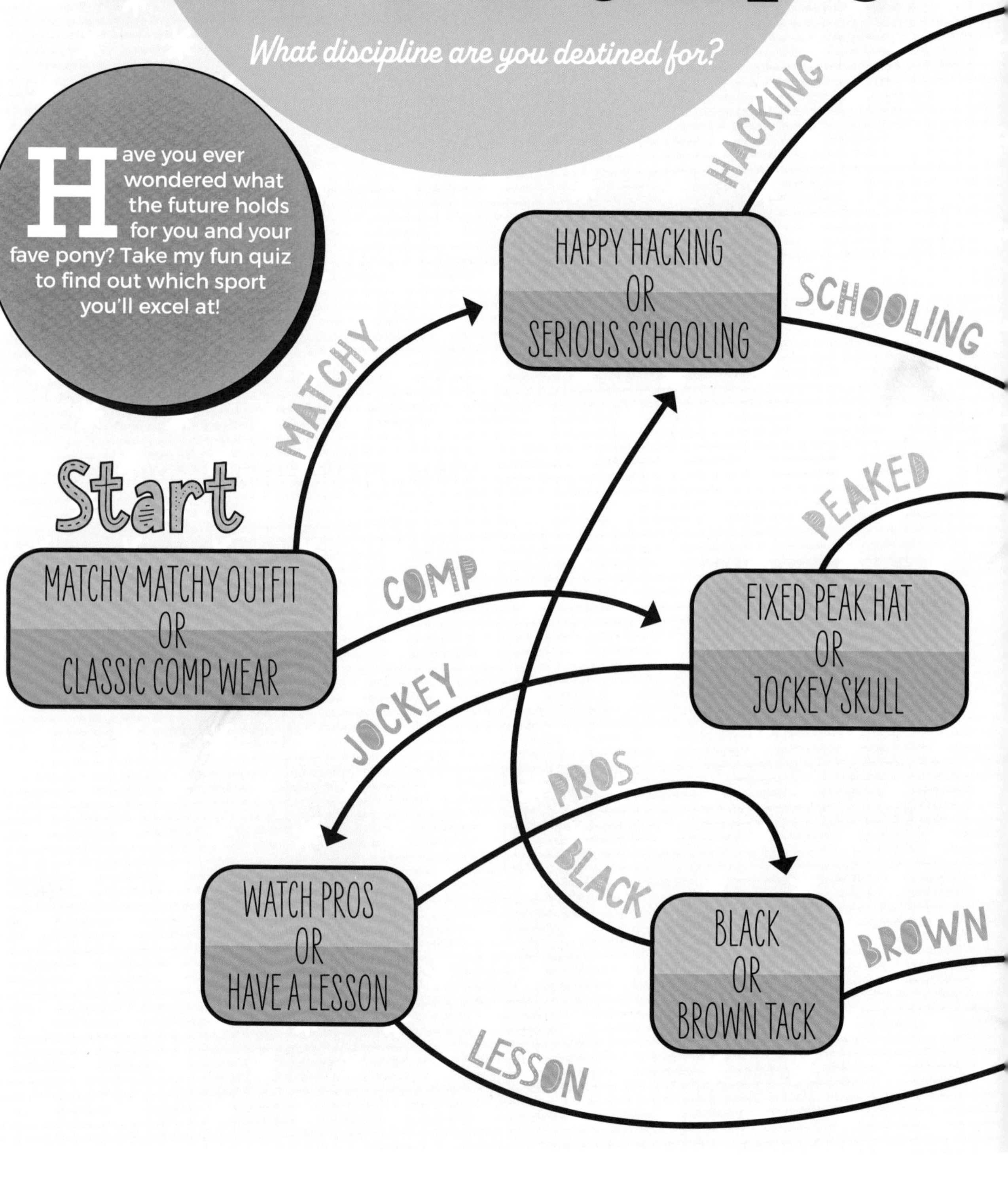

Start

MATCHY MATCHY OUTFIT OR CLASSIC COMP WEAR

MATCHY

COMP

JOCKEY

HACKING

HAPPY HACKING OR SERIOUS SCHOOLING

SCHOOLING

PEAKED

FIXED PEAK HAT OR JOCKEY SKULL

PROS

BLACK

WATCH PROS OR HAVE A LESSON

BLACK OR BROWN TACK

BROWN

LESSON

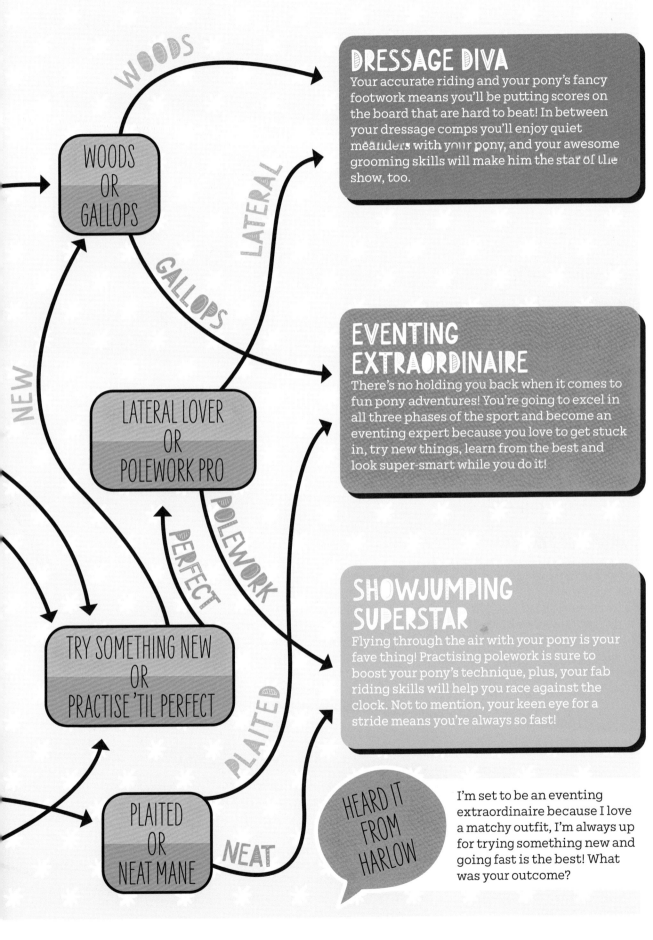

WOODS OR GALLOPS

LATERAL LOVER OR POLEWORK PRO

TRY SOMETHING NEW OR PRACTISE 'TIL PERFECT

PLAITED OR NEAT MANE

WOODS

LATERAL

GALLOPS

NEW

PERFECT

POLEWORK

PLAITED

NEAT

DRESSAGE DIVA
Your accurate riding and your pony's fancy footwork means you'll be putting scores on the board that are hard to beat! In between your dressage comps you'll enjoy quiet meanders with your pony, and your awesome grooming skills will make him the star of the show, too.

EVENTING EXTRAORDINAIRE
There's no holding you back when it comes to fun pony adventures! You're going to excel in all three phases of the sport and become an eventing expert because you love to get stuck in, try new things, learn from the best and look super-smart while you do it!

SHOWJUMPING SUPERSTAR
Flying through the air with your pony is your fave thing! Practising polework is sure to boost your pony's technique, plus, your fab riding skills will help you race against the clock. Not to mention, your keen eye for a stride means you're always so fast!

HEARD IT FROM HARLOW

I'm set to be an eventing extraordinaire because I love a matchy outfit, I'm always up for trying something new and going fast is the best! What was your outcome?

Why I love...
Riding bareback

It's a tricky skill to master, but has boosted our confidence and relationship so much!

Balance beam

Regularly riding bareback has done wonders for my balance and position! It can be tricky because I tense up my whole body when I feel unbalanced. But I've worked really hard on sitting up tall and straight, not relying on my hands and moving with Popcorn. It's definitely improved my riding skills!

Close contact

Riding bareback gives me a whole new perspective on how Popcorn moves when I'm on him. It's really amazing and interesting feeling how his muscles work and when he relaxes – and tenses up – which helps me understand how his body works during exercise sessions!

Up your game

As you feel more confident riding bareback you can try new things, which is super-exciting! At first, the thought of jumping Popcorn with no saddle on was so scary, but we slowly built up to it – starting with poles on the ground – and now we'll have a go at anything!

Trust test

We have to have so much faith that our ponies will care for us when we're on board, and this increases more when we ride bareback! The trust between me and Popcorn is always given a huge boost after a fun bareback session – it's so rewarding knowing he'll do whatever I ask.

Ultimate dare!

I love the adrenaline rush of doing riding dares and one of my faves is jumping bareback with no hands! I had to make sure Popcorn was really listening to my aids, but it was so cool and we even jumped a whole course! I was so proud of myself!

THE LOWDOWN

If you feel unbalanced, pop on a neck strap or hold onto your pony's mane for extra security. It's better to do this than pull on the reins and his mouth if you have a wobbly moment!

HEARD IT FROM HARLOW

Bareback pads were my saving grace when I was getting to grips with going saddle-free – they provide extra padding and more grip. So, if you're thinking about trying bareback riding, why not invest in a special saddle pad to help boost your confidence to start with?

It'll take time and plenty of practise before you feel confident and comfortable riding bareback. So don't rush to up the pace or jump – if you're not ready, you might bounce around a lot, which could make your pony feel sore.

JUMP WITH NO HANDS

Get ready to spread your wings while flying through the air!

What?

Jumping with no hands is when you put your arms out to the side as you fly over a fence. It's a super-cool challenge that'll test your balance and bravery!

The idea of flying over a fence without holding onto the reins might seem really scary and tricky, but it's so awesome when you can do it because it means you have loads of trust in your pony!

How?

Jumping's my absolute fave and upping the challenge by doing it without holding onto the reins makes it even more fun. When I'm ready and the jump's set up...

1. I approach the fence as normal, using my legs to keep Popcorn moving forwards and in a straight line.
2. I make sure to keep both hands on the reins all the way into the jump.
3. As Popcorn takes off, I lift both of my arms out to the sides – like a bird soaring through the air!
4. Then, I quickly bring my arms back down and pick up the reins as Popcorn lands.
5. I keep riding in a straight line away from the fence and give Popcorn a huge pat to say well done!

HEARD IT FROM HARLOW

Once I've warmed up Popcorn, I'll start by jumping the fence as normal (holding onto both reins) and before we try it with no hands, I knot my reins and jump it a few times with just one hand on the knot and the other out to the side.

⟶ THE LOWDOWN ⟵

Jumping over fences with no hands is a really useful exercise that encourages you to put your weight down into your heels, and not onto your pony's neck. It can help you to establish a balanced seat, which means your pony will find jumping much easier.

Fun

≋ TRY YOURSELF ≋

It's important to start off slowly so you don't knock yours and your pony's confidence. So, to start with, set up an inviting cross-pole that'll help keep your pony straight. It's a good idea to use guide poles on the ground, too, if you think your pony might run out at the last moment.

If you're feeling confident, why not increase the dare difficulty and have a go bareback or jumping all the way through a small grid without holding on?

MY FAVE
videos

Check out my top four vlogs so far!

With the number of vlogs on my YouTube channel increasing weekly, choosing my top four was such a tough decision! Which one of my videos would you pick as your ultimate fave?

Crazy pony at cross-country

As you guys know, I love XC and so does Popcorn! It was our second time at this venue and we planned to tackle some of the bigger jumps that we hadn't done before – how exciting! For once, we were early so I got my kit on while Popcorn chilled out and had a snack on some hay. It must've set us up for the day because Popcorn was amazing, even though at times he was mischievous and threw in some cheeky moves between fences! He jumped so well, though, and I loved every minute!

Riding dares challenge

This was an eventful vlog! We asked my Insta followers to set me and Lexi loads of dares and they didn't disappoint – all the ideas were pretty crazy! Probably the most scary one was cantering Popcorn without a bridle, and grooming blindfolded was the most difficult one for sure. Fifi and Popcorn were full of beans so the dares could've gone better, but we didn't fall off as much as we thought we would and we had so many giggles!

HEARD IT FROM HARLOW

After some behind-the-scenes action? Head to page 64! Don't forget to check out my YouTube channel, too, at **bit.ly/ HARLOW_YOUTUBE**

POPCORN'S BEST DAY EVER

Popcorn's best day ever

We took Popcorn to Cloudy's yard for the day and had a jumping lesson where we did lots of gridwork, which was so fun and really good for our confidence jumping bigger fences! We then went around the fields for a gallop and Popcorn was in full zoomies mode! It was the fastest I've ever galloped in my life, we reached a crazy 30mph – can you believe it? Riding through the gorgeous yellow fields was amazing, too, but my tack and boots were absolutely covered – lots of cleaning was required after our incred ride!

My first showjumping competition

My ultimate fave video so far has got to be our first showjumping comp. It was a cold and rainy day so Popcorn was wearing his cosy fleece rug, but the weather – and the fact we were running late – didn't dampen my mood! In the first class, Popcorn was a little spooky and it made me really nervous for the second class. Popcorn was phenom, though, and we jumped clear! I was sooo proud of him and it felt amazing, plus we got some gorgeous rosettes – winning!

MY FIRST SHOWJUMPING COMPETITION!

DREAMY DRESSAGE

Float through the paces to supercharge your dressage skills

Nailing the basics of flatwork will play a huge part in your dressage success! Did you know that it's the foundation to all riding activities, too?

Level one

Rhythm's one of the first things you learn when you start riding. It might feel tricky to master, but there are some easy methods I like to use to help. To get Popcorn into a consistent rhythm and keep it, I like to count the beat of each pace in my head, or I'll listen to my fave music to help me stay in time.

Tick when completed

Level two

It's really important that Popcorn's listening to all my aids and responds quickly to them. I practise lots of transitions at different markers, starting off with simple ones like walk to trot. Then I mix them up and increase the difficulty by doing walk to canter, for example. That's my fave transition, for sure!

Tick when completed

THE LOWDOWN

In a dressage test, you'll get marked on accuracy, your position and effectiveness as a rider, as well as your pony's gaits. So make sure you think about all these things while schooling to maximise your marks on the big day!

Level three

Riding lots of circles, turns and serpentines, as well as changes of bend, helps to supple up Popcorn and improve his balance. As I ride a turn, I use my inside rein to ask for the correct bend and my outside leg and rein to support Popcorn's shoulder to stop him from falling out around the turn.

Tick when completed

Level four

Impulsion's really key for showing off Popcorn's paces, so I practise shortening and lengthening his strides in all three gaits. To lengthen, I squeeze with my legs and open my rein contact so Popcorn can stretch out. To shorten, I sit deeper in the saddle and close my fingers around the reins.

Tick when completed

DRESSED
for the occasion

It's time to get dressed up for my five fave pony activities!

꞊Dressage꞊

Snaffle bridle

White saddle pad

White gloves

HEARD IT FROM HARLOW

I like to wear long boots, but you can wear short boots and jodhpur clips if you prefer!

ESSENTIALS!

For each discipline, Popcorn always wears a bridle, saddle and saddle pad and I'll wear my...

- riding hat ☐
- show shirt and jacket ☐
- white or beige breeches ☐
- long boots ☐
- gloves ☐

Then for every activity, we have some key accessories, and the other items in our wardrobe must be certain colours to suit the rules!

Cross-country

Matching fly veil and saddle pad

Jockey skull cap

Body protector

Baselayer

THE LOWDOWN

Check the rules for the sport you're doing to make sure what you've planned to wear is allowed. You don't want to arrive and find you're missing an essential item!

Short whip

Brushing boots
(you could use cross-country boots if you have them)

Jockey skull cap

Dark-coloured saddle pad

Long-sleeved shirt, PC tie and badge

THE LOWDOWN

Did you know that some disciplines have very strict limits on the length of your whip – for example showjumping and dressage. Make sure you measure yours to check it's allowed!

Short whip

≡ Pony Club ≡

⋛ Showing ⋛

Velvet-covered hat

Brown numnah

Long-sleeved shirt and tie

Jodhpur boots

Yellow gloves

⋛ Showjumping ⋛

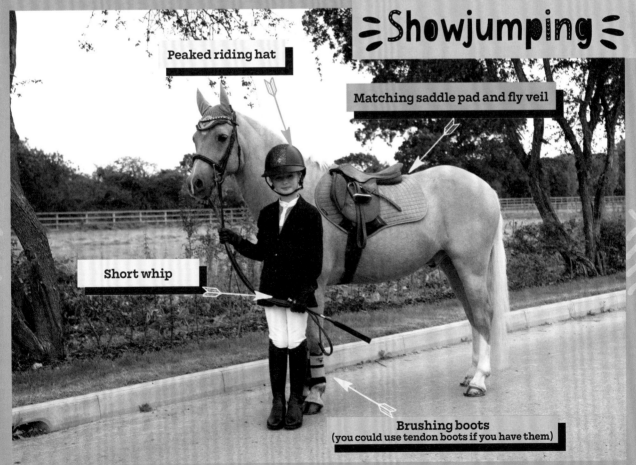

Peaked riding hat

Matching saddle pad and fly veil

Short whip

Brushing boots
(you could use tendon boots if you have them)

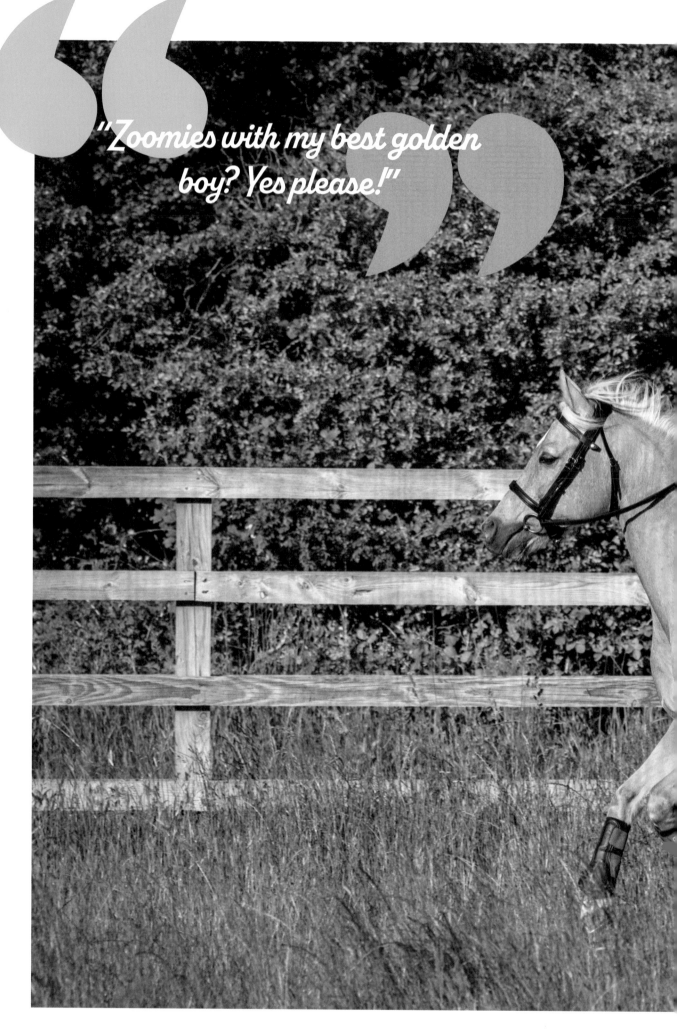

"*Zoomies with my best golden boy? Yes please!*"

On top of the the world

Make every schooling sesh amazing with my handy guide!

Want to know how to have an awesome session every time you enter the arena? Here's my plan that'll help set you up for success when you hop in the saddle.

1. Perfect prep

Setting myself achievable and realistic goals ahead of my session helps me progress my skills and makes me feel fantastic when I achieve them! Why not write down your aims and what steps you'll take to get there? It could be acing a new school movement, improving your position or tackling your nerves!

2. In the zone

Next, I follow my pre-ride routine on page 76 to get myself and Popcorn all geared up. I need to make sure I'm wearing comfy clothing that's suitable for the weather and activity I'll be doing – I don't want to get caught out in the rain without a jacket! Then, when I'm on board, I think carefully about my warm-up and how I can help Popcorn work at his best – I always focus on his rhythm and suppleness first before asking him for more.

3. Fully focused

It's time to get down to business! As I approach the main part of my session, I think about my goals and how I planned to achieve them. I start by riding the first exercise I've prepared for the session – thinking about how my aids are affecting Popcorn and what I need to do to improve. I don't expect everything to be spot on straight away – practise makes perfect, right?

THE LOWDOWN

We all have good days and bad days – it's what makes us human! So, don't worry if you're having a particularly bad day when nothing seems to go right. We all learn from our mistakes, and that way you're sure to nail it on your next try.

4. Press pause

It's super important to take breaks during schooling sessions – especially if you're doing a tricky or new exercise. I don't want to tire Popcorn out or make him sour by repeating something over and over again. If we're struggling with a certain activity, I'll try something different for a few minutes to take our minds off it. Then, when we go back to it, I'll have a clearer mind and a more positive approach.

5. Nailed it

I always finish each ride on a positive note, otherwise Popcorn might learn that he can get away with being naughty! I make sure I give him plenty of praise in the form of scratches and cuddles when he's done a good job. I also give him a long cool-down period to help him recover when we're done.

HEARD IT FROM HARLOW

Even if we're not filming for a vlog, I like to ask my mum to film snippets of my riding sessions so I can look back, check my progress and identify things that I could've done better. It's really helpful, whether I've had a great ride or a not so good one!

HAPPY HACKING

Follow these steps to boost your hacking confidence

Hacking's great for building your pony's bravery in unfamiliar places. Plus, it's sure to boost your bond together while giving you a great chance to blow away the cobwebs!

Level one

The best place to start if you feel nervous about hacking is at your yard! We don't have loads of hacking on our doorstep, so while I was getting my confidence up when I first got Popcorn, I just hacked down the track to the field. Doing it after a schooling session meant Popcorn was less excitable, too!

Tick when completed

Level two

When you feel ready to ride away from home, choose a quiet place – we took Popcorn for a hack in the woods. At first we just stuck to walk – I didn't want him to learn that he could trot and canter everywhere! My mum came along on foot, too, so she could lead Popcorn if I felt nervous, which was really reassuring.

Tick when completed

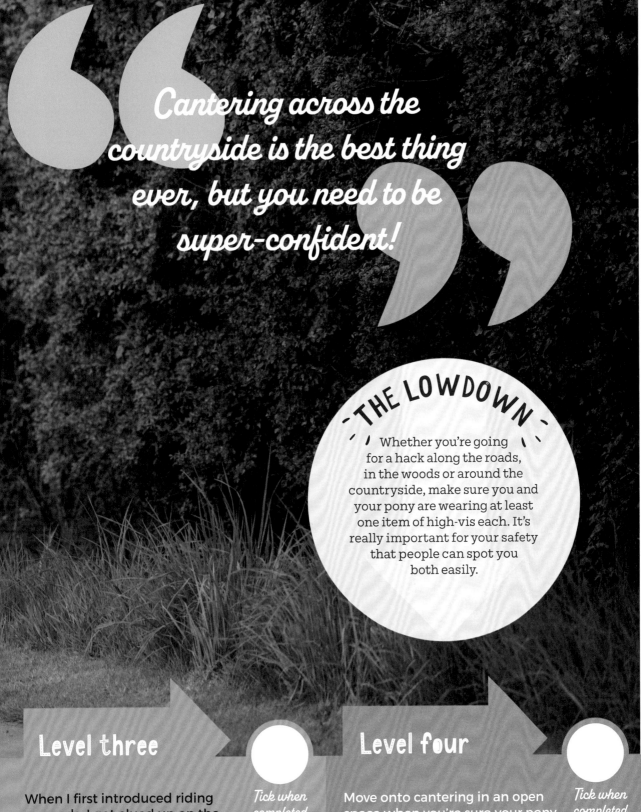

> *Cantering across the countryside is the best thing ever, but you need to be super-confident!*

THE LOWDOWN

Whether you're going for a hack along the roads, in the woods or around the countryside, make sure you and your pony are wearing at least one item of high-vis each. It's really important for your safety that people can spot you both easily.

Level three

When I first introduced riding on roads, I got clued up on the highway code to help keep us safe. Then I rode out with another pony who was really well-behaved and calm in traffic. When I felt nervous, we rode side by side or I went behind, but as I felt more brave, I led the way which was good fun!

Tick when completed

Level four

Move onto cantering in an open space when you're sure your pony will listen carefully to you. Popcorn gets excited easily when he canters with his friends, so if he doesn't listen or misbehaves I'll ask him to trot instead. Cantering across the countryside is the best thing ever, but you need to be super-confident!

Tick when completed

Why I love...
Pony Club camp

A week full to the brim of pony activities and fun with friends, Pony Club camp's the best!

Positive vibes

Having loads of riding and management lessons gives me such a confidence boost! I love being able to show my mum everything I've learnt and put it into practise when Popcorn and I get home.

Fun with friends

At Pony Club camp I get to have sleepovers with my friends every night and we always stay up late chatting about ponies, eating yummy snacks and dreaming of our next adventures! I feel sooo tired when I get home, but it's totally worth it!

Top of the class

I feel so proud when I get to add more rosettes and achievement badges to my collection. It's amazing to see all my hard work with Popcorn paying off and he always looks so pleased with himself, too!

Making memories

If Popcorn lived at home I'd be with him non-stop, and the most cool thing about camp is that I get to sleep near the stables, spend hours pampering Popcorn to make him look his best and even chill out in his stable. By the end of the week, our bond's stronger than ever!

Learning zone

It's great to be thrown in at the deep end once in a while and try something new! When you feel nervous, things can look scary, but at camp I'm encouraged by my instructor and friends so I have loads of guidance and support, which makes everything feel less daunting.

HEARD IT FROM HARLOW

When I start packing for a pony-mad week ahead I get sooo excited and the first day of camp just can't come soon enough! Writing a checklist for everything Popcorn and I need, then ticking it off as Mum helps me pack each item into the horsebox, helps me feel organised!

THE LOWDOWN

At camp you'll have two riding sessions every day, each lasting one hour. It's really important to spend time building your pony's fitness in the run-up to your week away so you can take part in all the activities.

THE LOWDOWN

If you're not feeling confident about staying away from home, you could attend a day camp instead! Just check with your local PC branch to see what's on offer.

BUBBLE BATH

Get your pony sparkling clean like Popcorn with my six-step guide to bathing!

Pony bathtimes are so much fun, and having a super-shiny pony is such a good feeling! Whether I'm getting ready for a competition or it's a gloriously sunny day and Popcorn needs a scrub up, here's how I get him bathed to perfection.

KIT CHECK

- ☐ hose or a bucket and water
- ☐ shampoo
- ☐ sponge
- ☐ curry comb
- ☐ stiff brush
- ☐ mane and tail brush
- ☐ sweat scraper

LET'S GO

1. First up, I grab the hose and rinse Popcorn's body all over.

2. Next, I apply shampoo to his body and legs – I like to squeeze it onto Popcorn's body, then massage it into his coat using my sponge. Then, I use a curry comb or stiff brush to help lift the dirt.

3. I squirt some shampoo onto his mane and tail, working through from the roots to the ends. Then, I use the mane and tail brush to get rid of any knots.

4. Next, I rinse Popcorn thoroughly until all the shampoo's out of his coat – making sure I double check all the bubbles are gone, otherwise they might irritate his skin when they dry.

5. To wash Popcorn's head, I add a dash of shampoo to my bucket of water and gently sponge his face. I take care not to get the bubbles in his eyes and ears because this might hurt him! Then, I rinse well with water and a clean sponge.

6. I grab my brush and, while running the hose over Popcorn's hooves, scrub his feet to remove mud and dirt – it's the ultimate finishing touch to get him sparkling!

THE LOWDOWN

Some ponies can feel nervous with the hose, so try using a bucket and sponge instead. Then slowly introduce the hose to him, starting at his legs and gradually working your way up his body each pamper session. Giving him a treat whenever he allows you to hose him will help boost his confidence, too!

Nailed it

Once the bathing session's done, I scrape off excess water from Popcorn's body and pop on a rug. Or, if it's a warm, sunny day, I take him for an in-hand graze in the sunshine to dry off.

HEARD IT FROM HARLOW

I try to avoid bathing Popcorn on chilly days so that he doesn't get cold! But if I'm going to a show, I'll only do the areas that need it and wash one part at a time with warm water. I'll also make sure the solarium is on because he loves it and it keeps me warm, too – bonus!

Meet Popcorn

FACT FILE

- **DATE OF BIRTH**
  9 June 2006
- **HEIGHT**
  13.2hh
- **BREED**
  Part-bred Welsh
- **BEST EQUINE FRIEND**
  Milo
- **FAVE TREAT**
  Carrots
- **FAVE ACTIVITY**
  Zoomies!
- **BEST COLOUR**
  Aqua

Popcorn's always been the cutest pony in the world (obvs). But did you know that, before we bought him, he had a really long mane all the way down to his shoulder? When we moved to our yard, we had his mane trimmed. Mum wasn't too sure at first, but it definitely makes him look extra smart!

Popcorn was once taught to drive a carriage! He's such a talented pony and has turned his hoof to so many disciplines!

TOP OF THE POPS

Aside from going zoomies at the gallops, Popcorn's fave thing to do is smiling! I find it hilarious when he lifts and curls his top lip – it's definitely his best trick! He loves splashing in the water, too. He used to be a bit nervous about it, but now he'll splash around at any given opportunity – whether we're in the sea, a pond or river!

The key to making Popcorn happy is to give him a really good scratch in his fave spot on his withers!

Insider info
When Popcorn's in the horsebox, he spends the whole time looking out the window! He's just sooo nosy!

"He's such a talented pony and has turned his hoof to so many disciplines!"

HEARD IT FROM HARLOW

Popcorn loves going out in the field with his best friend, Milo, and he marches all the way there! He's so good to bring in, though – we've never not been able to catch him!

HEARD IT FROM HARLOW

Popcorn's sooo cute when he's sleeping, but we don't see him lying down very often. If we're not at the yard and someone spots him snoozing, they'll video call us so we can see. It's totally adorable!

JOCKEY STIRRUPS

Switch into race mode and channel your inner jockey!

What?

Did you know that jockeys ride with really short stirrups so they can float above their horse's back, which means they can go faster more easily?

Staying out of the saddle requires sooo much strength and muscle, but pretending to be a jockey is really fun, and I love racing! Riding Cloudy has taught me loads and this challenge has certainly tested my skills!

How?

This dare is pretty tricky, so before I get into full jockey mode, I shorten my stirrups a few holes at a time, only putting them up when I feel happy. Making them too short too soon can lead to a wobbly moment!

1. When I'm ready, I start by sitting in the saddle and walking large around the arena.
2. On the long sides, I lift myself out of the saddle, keeping my knees bent, ankles flexed and bottom towards the back of the saddle.
3. As Cloudy walks, I allow my body to move with the motion, making sure I'm looking up and ahead.
4. Then, I gently sit back down in the saddle as I come onto the short side.

Doing it in short bursts helps to slowly build my strength without getting tired too quickly.

HEARD IT FROM HARLOW

My strength and balance has improved loads since I started riding Cloudy. But if I ever feel unstable, I hold onto his mane or a neck strap, rather than pulling on his mouth for support.

Riding with really short stirrups can put extra strain on your muscles and joints so, make sure you do lots of exercises out of the saddle that'll help to build your strength. Why not try wall sits, squats and lunges to get you started?

Fun

TRY YOURSELF

When your balance is on point, you can try it in trot and canter. Then, if you're feeling super bold, set up a start and finish line and race against your friends! Or you can up the challenge and set up small fences like the ones I jump when I'm training Cloudy – it's so fun!

Don't worry if you're finding it difficult, though. You could keep your stirrups long and practise standing up in them first before shortening them.

Squad goals!

What kind of yard friend are you?

Having loads of friends at the yard is the best thing ever because it means we get to have hours of pony-mad fun and go on cool horsey adventures and days out! But what type of yard friend are you? Take my quiz to find out!

2 You're spending the whole day at the yard. Are you more likely to...

A Go for a really long hack and chill out with your pony ☑

B Give the yard a spring clean ☐

C Help your friends with their riding lessons ☐

D Organise all your kit and check it's all in working order ☐

3 It's the morning of your friend's first competition. Are you more likely to...

A Go for a ride on your pony, but get back just in time to help her load ☑

B Muck out her pony for her ☐

C Groom and plait her pony for her ☐

D Let her borrow your comp checklist ☐

4 You've just got to the yard and your friend is having a jumping lesson. Are you more likely to...

A Sit down and watch the rest even though you missed the first half of the lesson ☐

B Poo pick the arena and stick around to clear the jumps away ☐

C Offer to change the heights of jumps so her instructor doesn't have to ☐

D Set up more jumps to build a course ☑

1 Your friend's had a fall and is nervous about getting back on her pony. Are you more likely to...

A Suggest she has a lesson ☐

B Tell her to get back on straight away ☐

C Let her ride your pony to build confidence ☐

D Offer to lead her around the arena ☑

6. You want to try a new hacking route. Are you more likely to...

A Go on an adventure – there's no point in planning ahead ☑

B Make sure your stable's super-tidy and all your kit's clean before you go ☐

C Look up the bridleways beforehand so you know where you're going ☐

D Print out a map and draw your route on it ☐

5. You're off on a horsey day out with a friend. Are you more likely to...

A Be so excited the night before that you can't sleep, and then oversleep! ☐

B Wake up extra early to get your ponies done before you head out ☑

C Pack a bag of snacks to share because that's the most important part ☐

D Look at the schedule and map ahead of the day so you don't miss a thing ☐

7. It's your best friend's birthday tomorrow and she's mentioned she wants to go for a fun ride. In the morning, are you more likely to...

A Just make it in time for the ride but haven't had time to get a card on the way ☐

B Still be grooming your pony to perfection ☐

C Do all her yard chores for her before the ride ☐

D Message all your other friends to arrange a surprise ☑

The results...

Count how many As, Bs, Cs and Ds you got. The one with the biggest number is what type of friend you are!

I'M THE...

The Late one

Mostly As

The late one

Whether you're having a lesson, hacking out with friends or heading off to a comp, you're often rushing around trying to get everything done – oopsie! But at least you don't miss out on the fun completely!

Mostly Bs

The tidy one

You're the neatest person on the yard – everyone's jealous of your clean and tidy field and stable, as well as your perfectly organised storage boxes for all your gear! Often, you'll be found tidying up after others, too, or sweeping every speck of dust off the yard – it's got to be immaculate!

It's 8pm and you're still at the yard. Are you more likely to be...

A Mucking out because you had a long ride earlier ☑

B Tidying up the yard because it was too messy ☐

C Helping your friend with her pony because she was running late ☐

D Making haynets for tomorrow – it's best to be prepared! ☐

Mostly Cs

The helpful one

You're always putting your fab friends first and your willingness to help them, even if it means getting less quality time with your pony, is so inspiring! It's great to have a yard friend like you, who will help put out poles, set up jumps or even tack up your pony for a lesson!

Mostly Ds

The organised one

You're so perfectly prepared that you're almost always ahead of schedule or, at worst, on time! Your organisational skills, and love for checklists, mean you can make loads of time for others because you were able to get all your yard chores done quickly and efficiently!

BEHIND THE SCENES

Dive into my world and see what I get up to on a vlog shoot!

I love planning and filming vlogs because I get to show you guys an insight into my life through my YouTube channel. But have you ever wondered what happens behind the scenes? Here's a sneak peek.

HEARD IT FROM HARLOW

I've got to make sure I keep my outfit clean, which is sometimes really hard work! It's so easy to get grubby around ponies and it's even harder to stay tidy if the video takes a while to do.

Brainstorming

First of all, my mum and I sit down and think about what sort of vlog we'd like to shoot. We go through loads of ideas and write them all down. We always base our vlogs on what I love doing with Popcorn, but they've got to be fun, too!

En route

I start most vlogs by chatting away to the camera in the car while we're en route to the yard. I don't follow a script, but sometimes if I get a bit carried away, my mum gives me a few prompts to keep me on track.

Star of the show

My mum has a special camera that she uses to film everything. It's pretty small so it's really easy to take into Popcorn's stable and other tight spaces like the back of the horsebox. Popcorn's amazing with the camera – he's such a natural – which makes our lives so much easier. Sometimes we have to do a few takes, but generally it's really easy and we get most things in one take.

Finishing touches

Once everything's been filmed, mum sits down and works her magic! She does all the editing at home on her computer, which can take her a while and I'm usually in bed and fast asleep by the time she gets round to it.

When she's finished putting the video together, I'll choose the cover for it and then we'll watch the whole thing back, thinking about the music and making any final adjustments so that it's perfect!

HEARD IT FROM HARLOW

My mum's a photographer so has loads of experience with the camera. She has an incredible eye for detail and she's amazing at getting the perfect shots of me and Popcorn. I couldn't do it without her!

Why I love...
Cross-country

Cruising around a cross-country course with Popcorn is just so much fun!

Perfect blend

Cross-country's the ultimate combination of our fave activities – cantering through the countryside and jumping! Not only is it the best of both worlds, but it also puts my riding skills to the test.

Slimline

Skinny fences can be sooo tricky, but I love the thrill of knowing I've nailed my approach and jumped it perfectly. Jumping skinnies puts our skills in the spotlight and it's so rewarding when our training pays off!

Looking good

As you guys know, I love matching with Popcorn, so choosing our XC outfit is always a tough decision! I'll wear a baselayer, riding tights and hat silk, and Popcorn will show off with his saddle pad and fly veil – all matching, of course!

Up and down

Jumping up steps feels weird at first because the landing phase is different, but it's so cool going up two or three in a row! I used to find jumping down steps really scary, but Popcorn's so good and always comes back to walk when I ask him so we can jump down carefully.

Challenge accepted

The ground conditions can vary loads out on the XC course. We have to keep an eye that it's not too hard or muddy, but riding up and downhill is really good for Popcorn's balance and fitness as well as mine!

HEARD IT FROM HARLOW

It's so important that you listen to your instructor about how to approach each fence on a cross-country course because it can vary between the different types of obstacles. Some will need a more open canter and others are all about straightness!

- THE LOWDOWN -

While you're warming up for a XC session, ask your pony for a more open canter and then practise shortening his strides again. It's essential you can do this out on course, so having a go in the warm-up will help set you up perfectly.

- THE LOWDOWN -

It's so important that you wear all the right safety gear. You'll need an up-to-standard jockey skull and body protector, as well as gloves and your usual riding gear. It's also a good idea to put boots on your pony to help protect his legs.

HAPPY HALLOWEEN

Check out my guide to making Halloween with your fave pony totally spooktacular!

All about him

Days spent at the yard playing ponies are the best, so here are some fun activities you, your pony and your friends can enjoy together on Halloween...

- create a dressage test to spooky music and ask your instructor to judge it – why not turn it into a whole yard competition and get everyone involved?
- teach your ponies some cool tricks, like smiling or bowing, and give them treats as a reward!
- organise a drill ride where you and your friends can showcase your epic Halloween outfits

HEARD IT FROM HARLOW

My local competition venue holds a special Halloween show every year where we can dress up and showjump – two of my fave things! Why don't you check out the schedule of your local venue? It's sure to be a really fun day out!

- hang white sheets over your jump blocks or wings to make them look like ghosts – spooky jumping sessions are go!

Get the look

Choosing what to dress up as for Halloween is such a tricky choice – there are so many different options! You could go for an easy Halloween look, such as a ghost, pumpkin or devil, or go all out and become a skeleton, zombie, witch or even a spider! Either way, adding colour and some cool details to your outfit is sure to make you stand out from the crowd.

OH, SO EXTRA!

Make your day even more mystical and mysterious by...

- carving pony-themed pumpkins – you and your friends could even make personalised ones to sit by your stables ☐

- painting your pony's hooves with glittery hoof oil to make them extra shiny ☐

- plaiting his mane, tail and forelock and securing them with colourful ribbons to spice up his look ☐

- adding a sparkly whip, boots and browband to give your outfit the wow-factor! ☐

A change of scene

Get to grips with riding different ponies to power up your skills!

Riding a new pony can be a nerve-racking experience, but did you know it can boost your confidence and teach you loads of new things, too?

Level up

Riding ponies who are experts in a range of disciplines has taught me loads! I've been lucky enough to ride racing Shetlands, polo ponies and even a FEI dressage pony, so my skillset is expanding, and I can't wait to try even more new things!

THE LOWDOWN

If you're feeling nervous, try to watch someone else ride the pony first. Getting to know his temperament, his way of going and how he likes to be ridden before getting on board will give you a huge boost.

Work it out

Riding other ponies can help you spot your strengths and weaknesses. You might find areas you need to work on, such as leg position or balance. When I first started riding Cloudy, I often felt unstable because he's so much smaller than Popcorn, but after doing loads of exercises to improve my balance, we have lots of fun together!

Change it up

You're sure to become a better rider, whether the new pony is strong, spooky, calm, or a schoolmaster! He'll help you to understand how and when to adapt your skills so you can boost his performance.

THE LOWDOWN

To get the most out of riding a different pony, why not ask your instructor for a lesson? Or, if you're feeling nervous, ask if you can swap at the end of your group lesson. It means you'll already be warmed up, feeling brave and ready to take on a new challenge!

A friend in need

It's really great having a friend like Lexi because if Popcorn misbehaves and knocks my confidence, we'll swap ponies! I hop on Jingles and get a huge boost when he looks after me, while Lexi helps get Popcorn back in the zone.

Familiar feeling

Riding another pony might make you appreciate your own even more – especially if the new pony is tricky or very different to what you're used to! This means you'll feel full of confidence and adoration when you get back on your equine BFF – and you'll be ready to take on anything!

Find your feet

Take your time when first riding a new pony. Rushing to try lots of new things, or pushing yourself too quickly, might knock your confidence. There are no set rules on when you need to achieve things by, so focus on enjoying it. After all, riding's meant to be about having fun!

HEARD IT FROM HARLOW

Watching someone else ride your pony – like when Lexi rides Popcorn for me – will teach you loads about how he moves under saddle and the things he likes or dislikes. This means you'll be able to get the most out of him when you get back on!

A day in my life

My life is nothing short of hectic! Find out what I get up to on a jam-packed weekday

It can be tricky – and a bit tiring – balancing my homework and horsey life, but with the help of my amazing mum, I get to squeeze in a ride on Popcorn most evenings after school. Here's what my typical day looks like!

6.45am

Time to start the day. My first thought as I switch off my alarm clock is about Popcorn, of course – I wonder if he slept as well as I did last night! I get ready for school and head downstairs for breakfast. When Mum makes pancakes I know it's going to be a great day!

7.30am

Mum waves me goodbye as I rush out the door just in time to get on the school bus! I can't help but think about Popcorn and what he's up to for the whole journey – I bet he's munching away in the field, greedy chops!

Ready for a busy day at school!

12.30pm

It's finally lunchtime after a long morning of lessons. Luckily, this afternoon we have PE, which I love, so I don't have to spend all day sitting in the classroom!

I've finally arrived at the yard!

4.15pm

Home time at last. I'm super-excited to see my fave boy – I hope he's had a fun day in the field with his friends!

"I'm exhausted, but already excited to see Popcorn tomorrow"

HEARD IT FROM HARLOW

Cloudy lives at a different yard so I see him as often as I can, but not as much as I see Popcorn. He's learning to race alongside the other Shetlands and does loads of hacking up hills as part of his training routine!

5.15pm

I manage to have some sneaky pony cuddles before sitting down to do my homework – best to get it done and out of the way so I can enjoy a fun ride!

5.45pm

Mum's tacked up Popcorn for me so I just need to zip up my boots, fasten my hat and hop on board. Sometimes we'll film a vlog, but tonight I'm practising my dressage test for the weekend!

I love bringing my toy ponies to life!

6.30pm

Popcorn was such a good boy tonight! He's back in his stable and enjoying his dinner – now I feel a bit hungry after our schooling sesh. While Mum cooks dinner in the yard kitchen, I play with my Schleich models and run through my dressage test on foot a few times!

7pm

Time to tuck Popcorn in for the night. I feel under his rug to check he's the right temperature and give him his night hay. He obviously gets lots of kisses and cuddles, too!

7.30pm

It's finally time to head home for a bath and bed! I'm exhausted, but already excited to see Popcorn tomorrow – maybe we'll go for a nice canter in the forest after school!

Good boy, Popcorn!

Ready, set, GO!

Learn how I set myself up for the perfect riding session every time

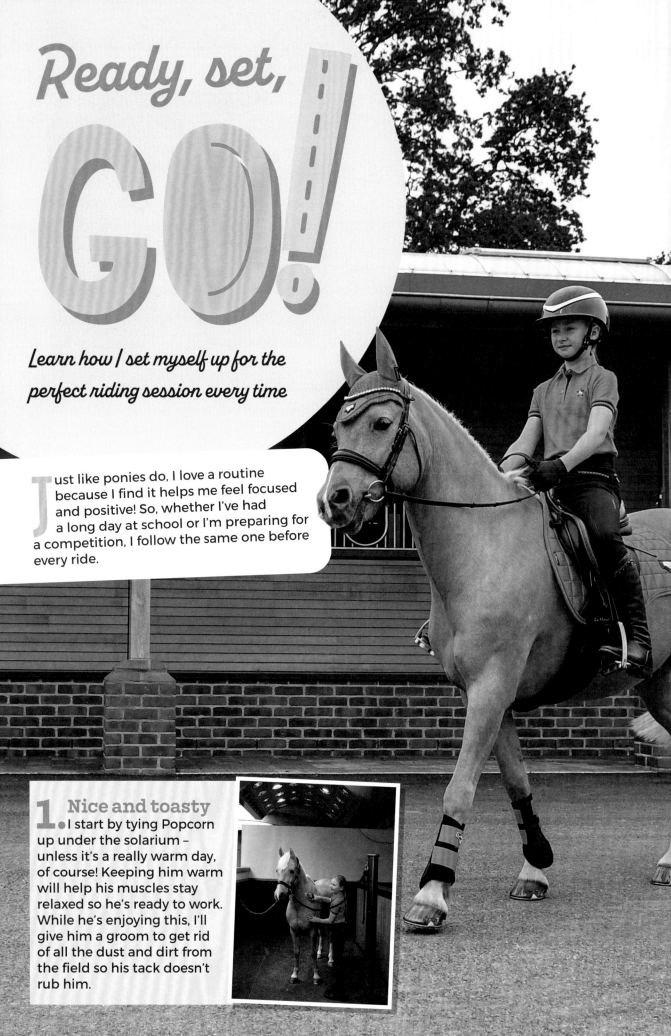

Just like ponies do, I love a routine because I find it helps me feel focused and positive! So, whether I've had a long day at school or I'm preparing for a competition, I follow the same one before every ride.

1. Nice and toasty
I start by tying Popcorn up under the solarium – unless it's a really warm day, of course! Keeping him warm will help his muscles stay relaxed so he's ready to work. While he's enjoying this, I'll give him a groom to get rid of all the dust and dirt from the field so his tack doesn't rub him.

2. Suited and booted

Boots are super important when it comes to protecting Popcorn's legs. The type of boots I put on him will depend on what we're up to – if we're going to be popping over some jumps, I'll usually put on his tendon and fetlock boots, but if we're just going for a chilled hack, he'll normally wear his brushing boots.

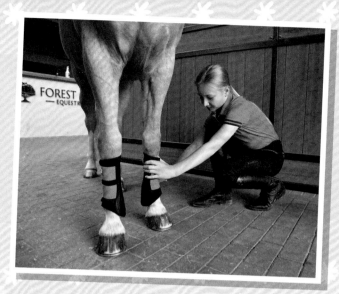

3. From the top

Putting on my safety gear is the most important part of getting ready to ride. My hat has got to match my outfit, so once I've chosen which one I'm wearing, I'll pop it on and fasten my chin strap. I then take off my wellies and hop into my riding boots and if I'm jumping I'll grab my body protector – then I'm all set to go!

4. Tool kit

It's time to tack up! I'll place Popcorn's numnah on his back before gently putting his saddle on and fastening up his girth. Then, I'll grab his bridle and put it on – checking all the buckles and straps are secure as I do each one up.

5. Open up

Even though we do our stretching exercises after each ride, before I get on I lift up Popcorn's legs and gently pull each one out in front of him. This helps to make sure the girth isn't pinching his skin, which would be super uncomfortable!

THE LOWDOWN

Did you know, stretching regularly can help to reduce your pony's risk of injury as well as improving his suppleness and flexibility? The best time to do lots of stretching exercises with your pony is after your ride because his muscles will be warmed up.

Nailed it

After checking my girth, I lead Popcorn up to the mounting block and hop on board. Now it's time to have some fun and we're both ready to get started with our schooling session or head off on another amazing adventure!

"*I literally adore a sunny hack with Popcorn, listening to his hoofbeats on the grass gives me goosebumps.*"

Challenge Harlow

JUMP BALES

Have a blast and try jumping something different!

What?

Whether it's bales of shavings, hay or straw, jumping something different at home is brill for your confidence and will help you tackle all sorts of spooky fences when you're out and about! Jumping single bales can boost your straightness, too, which is really useful whatever you do with your fave pony.

How?

I place a couple of bales side-by-side on the long diagonal over the centre line. Then, I grab two poles and prop them up on the bales to create an upside down V – these help guide Popcorn into the fence. When I'm warmed up and ready to jump...

1. I approach the bales in a punchy and positive canter, using my legs and voice to encourage Popcorn.
2. I keep my hands wide and low to channel him straight and in the middle of the V-poles.
3. As Popcorn takes off, I lift myself out the saddle, fold and give my reins slightly.
4. On landing, I ride away from the fence in a straight line and give Popcorn a scratch on his wither so he knows he's done a good job.

HEARD IT FROM HARLOW

Before I ask Popcorn to jump the bales, I spend time warming up around them, which allows him to have a good look. This means when it comes to popping over them he won't be fazed!

Riding dares can really help boost your confidence and ability, but make sure you always take things slowly and build up gradually. It's all about having a good time with your pony, so don't rush into anything if you're not ready!

Fun

TRY YOURSELF

Once you've tackled the bales a few times, take away the guide poles and see how you get on! Want to try an even trickier version of this dare? You could stand the bales on their end to make them taller – make sure you're already training at that height, though, otherwise you might get a confidence knock!

If you don't have any bales to jump, you could use rubber buckets or blocks instead. It'll be just as fun and still really challenging!

Make Memory board!

Show off all your wonderful pony moments with my easy make!

Looking back at the memories I've made with Popcorn, as well as all our incredible achievements, makes me feel so proud! My memory board's the perfect way to display all our fab horsey adventures, so why not make one to celebrate your own?

Kit check

- ☐ ruler
- ☐ 50x50cm soft wood frame
- ☐ pencil
- ☐ 20 hook screws
- ☐ ribbon
- ☐ pegs or clips
- ☐ rosettes, photos, dressage tests – whatever your best memories are!

Let's go

1. Use a ruler to measure out equal spaces (I did them 5cm apart) along each side of the frame on the inside, marking them with the pencil as you go.

2. Next, ask an adult to screw in the hooks where you've marked each point. Make sure they're in tightly!

3. Grab your fave-coloured ribbon and tie the end in a double knot around a hook.

4. Thread the ribbon through the hooks to create a random criss-crossing pattern – or you could do a neat design if you prefer – and secure the ribbon in another double knot around the last hook.

5. Gather all your mementos and use pegs or clips to attach each item to the ribbon. Make sure they're all spaced out so you can see them clearly!

6. Ask an adult to hang it up in your bedroom or tack room, so you can admire it and look back on all the good times whenever you want!

HEARD IT FROM HARLOW

Why not jazz up your memory board and use loads of different coloured ribbons, or paint your frame? You could also make a bunch of mini frames to showcase each awesome adventure that you and your pony have been on! It'll look phenom!

HORSEBOX TOUR

Want an exclusive tour of my epic horsebox?
Mum even customised the colours, so it's one-of-a-kind!

I love going on adventures with Popcorn and Cloudy, but Mum wasn't a fan of towing our trailer, and last year she decided to upgrade to a horsebox! She kept the design a total secret, so the day we picked it up was super exciting. Now we can go to stay-away shows – phenom!

OK, confession. It does take quite a lot of washing to keep it this clean. Thank goodness for Grandad and his pressure washer!

I love the giant logo on the side. I'll never lose it at a show, will I?! The horsebox's perfect for me, Mum, Popcorn and all our stuff.

HEARD IT FROM HARLOW

The inspo for the colour scheme was an ice cream van – check out all the cool pastel tones. I love them!

We've got all the creature comforts inside – including a mega comfy sofa, and Mum can even make me a hot chocolate between classes!

HEARD IT FROM HARLOW

There's a door from the living into the horse area, so I can chat to Popcorn while I'm getting ready. It's the best!

Popcorn and Cloudy each have their own lockers for their tack and accessories, so we never get mixed up!

Check out the gorgeous seats – definitely no muddy boots allowed in here!

Popcorn adores his new wheels – and I can watch him chomping his haynet on the camera in the cab. So cute!

Hit the target

Stay on track to complete your goals with my epic goal setting chart!

Plan of action

To get your hands on my goal setting chart, check out **bit.ly/HARLOW_GOALS** to download it and print out as many as you'd like!

If you're looking to try new things with your pony or working your way towards the dream of becoming a pro rider, you'll love my awesome chart. It's super-handy for helping you set goals, keep track of your progress and make you feel on top of the world when you achieve them!

I like to keep all my completed charts – and the ones in progress – in a special folder so they're all in one place. It means I can look back to see how far we've come, which helps boost my confidence if I'm having a tricky day!

GET SET, GO!

It's important to set goals that are SMART – they need to be specific, measurable, achievable, realistic and time-based. Here are some useful questions to ask yourself, as well as my handy tips to follow while you set your aims...

What exactly are you trying to achieve? Add in plenty of details to your aim.

How will you know when you're making progress? Set out clear steps to track your journey.

Is it possible for you to accomplish it? Make sure it's within your capabilities.

Is it relevant to your long-term objectives? Choose one that'll improve your all-round skills.

When do you want to achieve it by? Set yourself a time frame.

INSPO!

Struggling to come up with a goal or just want to add more to your list? Here are some ideas for you...

- ride a prelim dressage test
- go cross-country schooling and jump a ditch
- take your pony hacking somewhere new
- jump a 1m course
- qualify for the national championships
- jump five clear rounds

One of my goals is to compete Popcorn at a one-day event! I'm going to have loads of dressage lessons to help us prepare. Plus, we'll get out and about to put our skills to the test. Plenty of XC schooling is on the cards, too!

Meet Cloudy

- **DATE OF BIRTH**
  15 May 2009
- **HEIGHT**
  10hh
- **BREED**
  Shetland
- **BEST EQUINE FRIEND**
  Furby
- **FAVE TREAT**
  Polos
- **FAVE ACTIVITY**
  Galloping!
- **BEST COLOUR**
  Bluebell

Cloudy's the most tiny, adorable and competitive pony ever! The story of how we got him is a crazy one. Me and my mum took a horsebox when we viewed him because we just knew he was so perfect and he'd be coming home with us that day!

When Cloudy arrived home, we soon discovered his huge dislike for the hosepipe. Washing him was really hard, but he's not bothered by it now. He can be nervous with the farrier, too, and the first time he wore front shoes he walked as if he was on the moon – it was hilarious!

On cloud nine

I love riding Cloudy out with the other Shetlands, but my fave thing to do with him is jumping! He has a really bouncy canter and is sooo speedy, which makes it 10x more fun. He enjoys jumping on a long stride, too – that definitely puts my riding skills to the test, but at least he's got plenty of mane for me to hold onto!

Insider info

Cloudy was a stallion until he was 10 years old! He's even had babies – I can't begin to imagine how cute they are!

"It's my dream to race with Cloudy in front of the royal family one day"

HEARD IT FROM HARLOW

Cloudy does lots of hacking and hillwork as part of his training regime. He's so competitive and, although his trainer said it was unlikely we'd win a race in his first year competing, we won our first ever race together!

HEARD IT FROM HARLOW

It's my dream to race with Cloudy in front of the royal family one day. Racing at The London International Horse Show and Badminton are on my bucket list, too!

JOYFUL JUMPING

Fly high in the sky as you improve your jumping skills

Jumping's so much fun and your pony doesn't need to be the most agile or athletic to have a go. As you progress, your pony will build lots of muscle and become really strong, plus he'll love the exciting addition to his exercise routine!

Level one

Jumping cross-poles might seem easy, but they have so many great benefits. They look inviting, help keep Popcorn straight, and high-sided cross-poles can even improve his technique, too. As I approach in a positive canter, I widen my hands slightly to channel Popcorn to the centre of the jump.

Tick when completed

Level two

Even though uprights look different to cross-poles, I ride them in exactly the same way. First, I make sure I have a really straight line on the approach to help set up Popcorn so he jumps the middle. Then I focus on looking up and over the fence, rather than down, because that might encourage him to refuse or chip in an extra stride.

Tick when completed

THE LOWDOWN

While you're building your confidence, keep the fences low and use plain poles and wings that won't spook your pony. It's not about jumping as high as you can, it's about feeling good and having fun while you're doing it!

Jump guide!

Cross-pole

Upright

Oxer

Level three

Oxers might seem daunting because they're much wider than uprights, but they're really fun to jump! They help Popcorn build strength in his quarters and encourage him to make a nice shape in the air – V-poles can help teach him to lift up even more, too. Having a canter with lots of impulsion is key when jumping oxers!

Tick when completed

Next level

When you're feeling extra confident jumping around a course of fences, why not try practising some jump-off turns? Picking up the pace, cutting corners and jumping on an angle will be a true test of your skills!

Level four

Whether it's doubles, grids or in a course, jumping fences in a row doesn't change how I ride each one. Planning each approach and making sure I keep a positive canter helps me to jump clear every time. Keeping my eyes on the next fence to encourage Popcorn to land on the correct lead helps us jump round smoothly, too.

Tick when completed

Celebrate

HAPPY CHRISTMAS

Spread some festive cheer with your fave pony and make it the most wonderful time of the year!

All about him

It's almost the end of the year, so why not treat your pony to some extra-special goodies and celebrate your amazing achievements? To show him how much he means to you, you could...

- buy him a horsey advent calendar that's full of his fave snacks – or make him one so you can include a range of treats!
- give him a Christmas Eve box with an extra ration of carrots inside
- make him a personalised stocking
- draw him a Christmas card and include your best photo of you both together

- save up your pocket money and treat him to a new bridle, pair of boots or headcollar!

Get the look

Either keep it simple with a Christmassy matchy set – including a hat silk, baselayer, fly veil and saddle pad – or give it everything you've got and don't hold back! You could go full elf mode or pop on a crown and cloak to become one of the three wise men! There are easy ways to get your pony into the Christmas spirit, too. Add a pair of antlers or dress him up in red and green!

HEARD IT FROM HARLOW

Why not organise a fun-filled and festive afternoon of games and races to kick off the Christmas season in style? You could award prizes or rosettes for the best dressed and then enjoy some yummy snacks to celebrate!

OH, SO EXTRA!

Go crazy at Christmas and get into the ultimate festive mood by...

- decorating your stable, tack or jumps with tinsel! ☐
- leaving a carrot out for Rudolph – the ponies will be so excited to meet him when Santa swings by the yard! ☐
- going out for a hack and singing carols along the way ☐
- setting up a naughty or nice scale and rating your pony's behaviour – obviously Popcorn's always on the nice list! ☐

Riding

Pretty plaits

1. Divide your hair into two bunches. Then split the first bunch into three sections ready to be plaited.

2. As you plait down, keep a firm, even grip so the plait isn't too loose, otherwise strands of hair will come out and look messy!

Beautiful bun

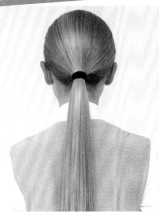

1. Start by brushing through your hair and tie it in a neat, low ponytail.

2. Divide your hair into three sections and plait all the way down to the bottom.

hair

Polish off your competition outfit with my stunning hair styles!

3. As you get to the bottom of each plait, secure it with a hair band – make sure it's really tight!

4. Secure the ribbons at the end of your plaits – now you're ready to dazzle in the show ring!

3. Wrap your plait around itself, securing hair grips as you go to keep it in place.

4. Pop your scrunchie over your bun for the ultimate dressage diva look!

Why I love...
beach rides

Sun, sand and sea are the perfect combination for an amazing adventure

Popcorn can get nervous about going into water, so I'll ask my friend to lead us in to help boost his confidence and I give him lots of praise at the same time. Walking through shallow water is so good for his muscles, too.

Freshen up

What's better than a trip to the beach on a hot summer's day to cool down? As Popcorn paddles along the shore, I can feel the water splashing my legs and it's sooo refreshing.

Amazing scenes

The beach is the perfect place to have a photoshoot with your pony! Some of my fave pics of me and Popcorn are from our beach adventures. The colourful horizons and sandy shores set the most gorgeous scene!

Best of friends

Your first ride on the beach can be a bit daunting, but once it's over you're sure to want to go again! Beach rides allow you to bond even more with your pony and build on the trust that you've already got between you.

Zoomies

I love looking through Popcorn's happy ears and feeling the wind in my hair as we canter across the sand. When I allow my hands forwards and let him open up his stride, it's such an exhilarating moment!

Always learning

Riding on the beach has encouraged Popcorn to become really brave with water – which helps when we're out on the cross-country course – and it's even boosted our confidence in open spaces, too.

THE LOWDOWN

If you're planning a beach ride, make sure you check any rules about when and where ponies are allowed on the sand – and don't forget to look up the tide times so you don't get caught out!

Cameras at all angles!

Posing with my superstar pony!

How we made the yearbook

We had so much fun
behind the scenes!

Browband goals!

Peter the photographer looking phenom!

I can't believe it snowed in April!

Guys, arena surface is sooo sticky!

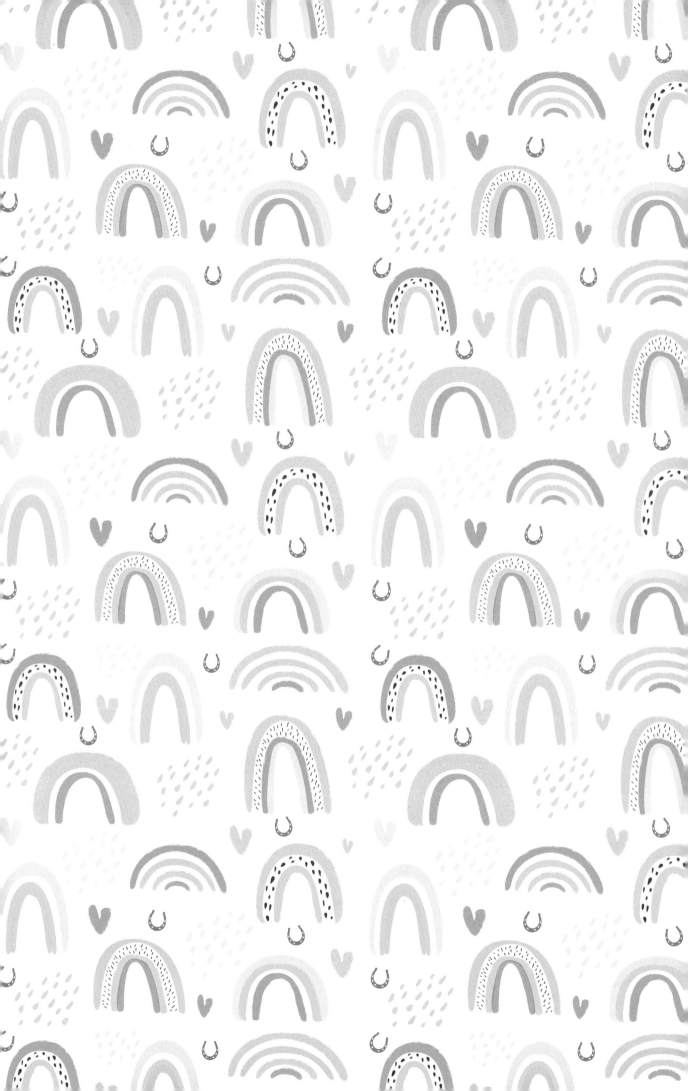